My Human Experience

Storm Brooks

Copyright © 2024 Storm Brooks
All rights reserved
First Edition

PAGE PUBLISHING
Conneaut Lake, PA

First originally published by Page Publishing 2024

ISBN 979-8-89315-314-9 (pbk)
ISBN 979-8-89315-320-0 (digital)

Printed in the United States of America

ENEMY

I wish I had said, "Don't go, don't leave. I can do better than this, you'll see. This isn't who I am, this isn't me. So don't go, please."

I wish I had grabbed your arm as you turned to leave. I wish I had pulled you in close, kissed your cheek, and begged you not to leave.

I'm sorry about this, about the person you've seen. The person I've been—that girl, she's not me. I'm my own worst enemy, and I'm so sorry.

LITTLE REMINDERS

It's the littlest things that make me think about you
Like Drumsticks and midnight and anything blue
Oh, and kittens too
Like Netflix and stars
The solar eclipse
The empty side of my bed, the emptiness on my lips
Like the taste of rum as it trickles down
The feeling I get when you're not around
Like the smell of your cologne that still hangs in the air
And the great memories I can no longer bear.

THE BOAST (INSPIRED BY "BEOWULF")

I am proficient in the art of silent speech.

A master of words, commander of language, and the ruler of verse.

My poetry is splendid—worthy of recognition, worthy of divulgation.

The elegance of each poem will leave you breathless and in awe, amazed and astonished by the pure prowess presented in every line.

My short stories are showstoppers that will take your breath away and leave you on the edge of your seat as you cling to every word, mesmerized, and magnetized by their beauty.

There is not a wordsmith alive whose works will ever surpass the greatness of my own.

My compositions will be remembered and renowned by people for generations to come.

The majesty of my writing cannot be surpassed by any others, living or dead.

Not even the works of Poe, Frost, or even Shakespeare can compare.

My work will go down in history.

You will remember me forever.

BEST MEDICINE

I loved a girl with all my heart
She made me want to live
She was the best medicine
She gave me all she had to give
I loved a girl with all my heart
She made me feel complete
She was the best medicine
She willed my heart to beat
I loved a girl with all my heart
She made me feel alive
She was the best medicine
She made happiness thrive
I loved a girl with all my heart
She really believed in me
I wanted to marry her
But now she's six feet deep

PRAYERS AND NOTES

The letters are ready.
They're waiting downstairs.
Delicately folded, addressed mostly in pairs.
Mom and Dad,
Hunter and Bailey,
Kim and Savannah,
I pray they won't hate me.
My sons are too young to know what this means.
I've made them a video so they'll always have my voice and a screenshot of me.
Maybe somebody will show them pictures of when I was happy.
When was I happy?
I can't remember the last time before today.
I'm relieved at my decision to no longer stay.
I usually don't pray
Except today.

PILLS

I hold the pills in my hand
Steady, confident, ready.
The shakes have subsided; my mind is already decided.
I'm not sorry.
I can't help but think what comes next for me.
Will I fall asleep before my heart stops beating?
Will I be in agony, regretting everything as I struggle with breathing?
The pills stare back at me.
I'm not sure if this will work.
How many pills do I need to succeed?
A handful, a bottle?
Maybe everything?
I add a few more to the pile already staring at me.
What am I doing?
I don't have time to second-guess this.
On the count of three,
Steady, confident, ready.
One,
Two,
Three,
I'm so sorry.

FALLING

As a heap of tangled limbs, we lay
Side by side at the end of the day
The love we have can't be undone
You and me,
Together as one

I WILL LOVE YOU ALWAYS

At first, I started at the sight.
Tears welled up in my eyes, afraid of what this meant for me.
Two pink lines, I couldn't believe.
The tears did stop eventually.
A thought formed in my mind:
"I will love you always."
Long days became sleepless nights.
Anticipation became delight.
I watched you grow like a flower in spring,
Thinking all the while,
I will love you always.
If there should come a day when I'm no longer by your side,
Please find comfort in knowing I'll never leave you behind.
I'll hold you forever in my arms and heart as I have from the very
   start.
I will love you always.

COSMIC DESIGN

I am stardust and atoms, cosmically beautiful and made of magic.

The universe swirls in my veins like a story waiting to be told, like a dandelion carrying the weight of one's soul.

The wind whispers secrets for only my ears to know—secrets on how to be brave and kind and bold like the trees are as the seasons come and go.

Restlessly waiting for something not yet known because the universe has plans for this and that and those, a plan for everything it grows.

After all, the universe should know.

It was there when I was made, spoke life into my bones.

Cradled me so gently, marveled at my heart, then decided I was a perfect piece of art.

At least that's what I thought when I was younger, but now, I can't help but wonder what you see when you look at me.

When you look at me, I wonder if you can tell that I am broken.

Nothing more than a hollow shell of the girl I used to be—the one who laughed too loudly at even the smallest of things.

I wonder if you can see the ghosts that haunt me or if I do a good enough job at keeping them locked behind this cage made of teeth.

Does my smile betray me?

If you could see the demons I'm fighting, would you still call me pretty?

Even when you know they are fights that I'm losing?

Even when I emerge from them bruised and bloody, my mind a graveyard for all things happy?

And if you could see the monsters in the closet, what would you think of me then?

Would you call me crazy?

Look at me with pity?

Would you wonder how I manage to hide such hideous beasts?

When you look at me, I wonder if this is what you see.

And if it is, I wonder how you could ever want me.

When I look in the mirror, my depression says to me,

"I am the ice you are trapped beneath.

No matter how hard you struggle, you will never break free."

I wonder why you were drawn to me.

Is it because on the surface I seem calm and serene?

If only you could see the waves crashing against the surface, dying to break free.

There is something wrong inside of me.

Would you have run if you had known that the place I call home is a wasteland?

Not capable of producing fruits and greens, nothing vibrant grows here.

No roots dare to plant themselves in my soil because they know it is eternally winter here and they will never make it through the night.

No, I am not anybody's home, not even my own.

So please, just go.

Leave me and my demons alone in our frozen wasteland,

The brain and body I call home.

PRETENDING (WHO AM I KIDDING?)

I want you to hate me
At least then, leaving would be easy
Spend every day watching me disappear,
Lost in my own head,
Addicted to the drama,
Just to feel anything
Push you away again
Gotta learn to let you go
Sitting by the phone
Waiting for it to ring
Another night without your call
Another night to let the loneliness devour me
So I crawl into the shower, hoping to escape
Pretend the warm water is your skin pressed against mine and we're
    fine
The way it used to be
Who am I kidding?

LOSING ME

Lately,
I feel so lost, so alone
No place to go,
No place to call home,
Half dead,
Lying in bed.
All my friends left on read.
Promises broken.
Commitments ignored.
I feel like a zombie.
I am getting bored.
Feeling like this used to remind me that I am alive
And of what it means to be happy.
Now I long to feel anything,
Anything other than the horrible sinking.
I am drowning,
Lost in the open,
Lost in a crowd,
Longing for silence, but the world's too loud.
No relief,
No way out,
Emptiness all around.
Lately,
That is all I have found.

HOUDINI

Don't come looking for me if I disappear
The girl you're searching for won't be there
She's so far away, lost in her own mind
Like an inescapable maze, she's trapped for all time
We may never get her back
She's Houdini, and this is her final act

SHADOWS AND SANDCASTLES

A shadow of you
I used to love
Stands against a distant shore,
Faded and blurry—
Not who you were,
Not who I want anymore.
Like a sandcastle,
I'm washed away
By the memories of us.
They flood my thoughts,
Strip away my sanity
Until the only thing that's left is desperately wanting you to bury me on this beach.

PTSD SEASON

Strong voices falling silent,
Steady hands shaking,
Losing hope, losing touch,
Giving up—
Lungs empty,
Heart not beating—
Strength is silently retreating,
Losing hope, losing touch,
Giving up—
Numbness settles in.
Here we go again.
Another day,
Another week,
Another month,
Losing hope, losing touch,
Giving up.

VOID

Hi,

It's me, the Void, calling. It's been a while since we last spoke. I knew you couldn't ignore me forever, though. You always run back to the things that feel like home.

SINNERS

Indulging makes us abandon all but our own pleasures and desires.
Lust and greed for you fuel my fires.
Are we wicked for feeling good?
We're sinners, me and you.

LOVE, SUNFLOWER

When the days are bleak, you make them bright,
My own personal ray of sunlight
Your honey-soaked eyes say, "Everything will be alright"
Your touch keeps me safe throughout the night
With you I'm so happy, I can't deny
Your kiss makes me feel like I can fly
I swear your love could get me high
My feelings for you will never die
This poem is cheesy;
I'm sure you agree
I wrote it to ask,
"Will you marry me?"

MISTRESS

Writing always was my one and only true love;
Now she's my mistress,
Always out of reach—
A promise I couldn't keep.
Pens all out of ink.
The one that got away—
I miss her every day.

WAY OUT

You are looking for a way out
You do not have to pretend
I see it in your eyes when we start to fight again
I hear it in the music you listen to
The words in those songs hurt me
They do not seem to bother you

LONG DISTANCE

When you were here, everything was fine
I had all I needed right by my side
Finally, I got to look you in the eyes
I swear I fell more in love each time
Day turns to night
Night turns to day
I just watch as the hours pass by
I can't keep living behind these screens
Being so far from you is killing me
I sit all alone
Why does time move so slow?
My heart's missing you
What am I supposed to do?
There's an ache in my chest,
A hole I can't fill
I should've run away with you when I could
Day turns to night
Night turns to day
Being so far from you is killing me,
But I swear I'll be home soon

ODD ONE OUT

It's always me,
The odd one out.
The friend for convenience
But never sought out.
Left behind every time
For someone exciting, different, new,
More normal too.
I'm at peace when I'm alone.
I have to be; it's all I've known.
But once,
Just once,
It would be nice to be included,
Invited,
Wanted,
Instead of the odd one out again.

CONCEPTION

My eyes are open;
I'm wide awake.
The nightmare begins;
I start to shake.
It's like a bad dream in the middle of the day;
He's not here, but I feel his hands on me.
I start to cry
And beg
And plead
"Please, why are you doing this to me?"
I want to scream, but all that comes out is a whimper
He thinks it's a moan.
Faster and faster and faster he goes,
Taking what he wants, not caring what I need.
With his hand clamped over my mouth, I can barely breathe,
Exactly how he likes me.
My body is tired.
Everything hurts.
I'm sore, I'm empty.
I wonder if he'll be done soon.
He threatens me with pregnancy.
I want to scream.
He finishes inside of me.
My eyes are open;
I'm wide awake.
The sun streams in; it's the middle of the day.
He's not here, nowhere to be found.
I see a pair of eyes, big and round.

A small voice whispers from the bed near me,
"Good morning, Mommy."
And I know we're safe.

DESTRUCTION

Our love
Is like a wildfire,
Burning out of control.
I know that I should go.
I'm having too much fun,
So I stay
And continue this dangerous game.

HAIKU FOR LUST

Your hands, my body
I shiver with ecstasy
Need you inside me

UNRELIABLE

I've determined poetry is an unreliable art.
Why is it I can only write when falling in love or falling apart?
When I try to write it just feels fake
Sitting at the computer, hoping the words take.
I make another mistake;
I decide I need a break.
I get up,
Slam the computer shut,
And take a nap instead.

ANGER

I'm sorry about what I've become
All I want to be is numb
All I feel is this anger
I'm not sure where it's coming from
The longer it's there, the more it seems unfair; how useless and cruel
    the world can be
All I ever wanted was to see my sons grow up,
Feel that sense of pride,
But all I ever feel is dead inside

ETHER

If I disappear into the ether, just know I didn't want to be there
Amidst shadows deep, lost where silence gently weaves through the
    secrets that we keep
Does my heart still beat?

SAILS

On a sailboat
In the sea
Drifting endlessly
No direction
No place to be
Nobody to need me
Exactly how it should be

COLD FEET

In the midst of vows, a haunting doubt unfurls
A heart's once vivid beat now faintly swirls
Amidst the plans for futures intertwined, a whisper of unrest within the mind
The path once clear now veiled in misty doubt
Feelings once ablaze now flicker,
Falter,
Flout
Promises poised on the edge of hollowed dreams
Echoes of love now torn at the seams
An ache, a shift
As love begins to wane
An inner storm, a tempest brain
The knot that binds now frayed
A realization that love's bloom is no longer worn
Courage stirs amidst the heart's decline
To halt the march toward vows once made divine
For truth, though harsh, demands its rightful space
To salvage hearts from love's fading embrace
In letting go, a bittersweet release
Shadows linger; whispered woes decrease
For in the space where love no longer thrives lies hope for newfound joy in separate lives

SOUTHERN SUMMERS

In the sultry embrace of southern skies,
Whispers of summer in every sigh.
The air like a blanket of warmth and sound,
Cicadas humming all around.
Fireflies dance in the humid air,
Their flickering lights a cosmic affair.
Moonbeams paint the magnolia blooms;
Stars wink through the jasmine's perfumed plumes.
Front porches creak with tales untold
As sweet tea's sipped stories unfold.
Gentle winds carry melodies afar,
Strumming guitars beneath the stars.
Families gather, laughter's embrace
Underneath the vast celestial space.
Southern summer nights, a tranquil sight,
Where memories linger, soft and bright.

HAIKU FOR INNOCENCE

Dancing lights at dusk
Children chase in twilight's hush
Fireflies in their clutch

I WISH I COULD HATE YOU

She looks at me with bloodshot eyes
No one knows how hard she cries
No one knows that every night she thinks of ways to say goodbye,
Not just to me but to her life
That smile she wears is just a lie
She's dreaming of the day she dies
She's smiling while planning her own demise,
A short and simple suicide
She imagines what they all will think
When they find her body in the lake—
Floating, lifeless, like her eyes when she looks at me and gives me one
    last kiss goodnight
Those lifeless eyes still haunt my dreams
I miss her whispering, so soft and sweet
I miss the way she kisses me and holds me while I fall asleep
I miss the way she used to sing
My sunshine's what she stole from me that night she "went to sleep,"
Taking all my hopes and my dreams
And ripping my heart apart at the seams
The joy I felt,
The laughs we shared—
They didn't matter
This isn't fair
Did she ever even care?

ABOUT THE AUTHOR

Storm is a passionate advocate for mental health awareness, utilizing poetry as a tool for catharsis and connection. Through *My Human Experience*, Storm aims to shine a light on the often isolating experience of PTSD, offering solace and solidarity to those who feel alone in their struggles.

Printed in the USA
CPSIA information can be obtained
at www.ICGtesting.com
CBHW031624150824
13252CB00011B/429